THE EMPIRE OF FORGETTING

BY THE SAME AUTHOR

POETRY

The Hoop
Common Knowledge
Feast Days
The Myth of the Twin
Swimming in the Flood
A Normal Skin
The Asylum Dance
The Light Trap
The Good Neighbour
Selected Poems
Gift Songs
The Hunt in the Forest
Black Cat Bone
All One Breath
Still Life with Feeding Snake
Learning to Sleep
Ruin, Blossom

NON-FICTION

A Lie About My Father
Waking Up in Toytown
I Put a Spell on You
The Music of Time: Poetry in the Twentieth Century
Aurochs and Auks

FICTION

The Dumb House
The Mercy Boys
Burning Elvis
The Locust Room
Living Nowhere
The Devil's Footprints
Glister
A Summer of Drowning
Something Like Happy
Ashland & Vine

THE EMPIRE OF FORGETTING

John Burnside

CAPE POETRY

3 5 7 9 10 8 6 4 2

Jonathan Cape, an imprint of Vintage, is part of the
Penguin Random House group of companies

Vintage, Penguin Random House UK, One Embassy Gardens,
8 Viaduct Gardens, London SW11 7BW

penguin.co.uk/vintage
global.penguinrandomhouse.com

First published by Jonathan Cape in 2025

Copyright © John Burnside 2025

The moral right of the author has been asserted

Penguin Random House values and supports copyright. Copyright fuels creativity, encourages diverse voices, promotes freedom of expression and supports a vibrant culture. Thank you for purchasing an authorised edition of this book and for respecting intellectual property laws by not reproducing, scanning or distributing any part of it by any means without permission. You are supporting authors and enabling Penguin Random House to continue to publish books for everyone. No part of this book may be used or reproduced in any manner for the purpose of training artificial intelligence technologies or systems. In accordance with Article 4(3) of the DSM Directive 2019/790, Penguin Random House expressly reserves this work from the text and data mining exception.

Typeset in 11/13pt Bembo Book MT Pro by Jouve (UK), Milton Keynes
Printed and bound in Great Britain by TJ Books

The authorised representative in the EEA is Penguin Random House Ireland,
Morrison Chambers, 32 Nassau Street, Dublin D02 YH68

A CIP catalogue record for this book is available from the British Library

ISBN 9781787334557

Penguin Random House is committed to a sustainable future
for our business, our readers and our planet. This book is made
from Forest Stewardship Council® certified paper.

enfin, l'empire de l'oubli, qui est un empire divisé entre l'effacement définitif des traces et l'oubli de réserve, celui qui donne l'assurance qu'une anamnèse est possible.
Paul Ricoeur

*There are no stars tonight
But those of memory.
Yet how much room for memory there is
In the loose girdle of soft rain.*
Hart Crane

CONTENTS

Foreword	ix
Notes towards a *Devotio Moderna*	1
Notes towards a *Wächterlied*	6
Winter Sutra	7
The Memory Wheel	8
A Theory of Siberia	13
The Empire of Forgetting	14
Last Days	16
To the Old Gods	17
Nature Study	19
Variations on 'The Ruin'	20
A Variation on 'Panis Angelicus'	24
A Variation on 'Auld Lang Syne'	25
A Recusant	26
The Elders	27
Folk Story	30
October 2023	31
As if from the End Times	32
God Bless the Child	33
Listen with Mother	34
Notes & Acknowledgements	43

FOREWORD

This is the last collection of new poems by John Burnside, and our thirtieth book together. Whether John considered it finished we cannot know, but these are the poems that exist. He had told me it was close to completion and we had started discussing possible cover approaches. In March 2024 – on what I now realise was his 69th birthday – he emailed some familiar images by Magritte and De Chirico, but finished by adding 'if we felt we could prevail on Tim again, that would also be great'. John had loved the covers for *Aurochs and Auks* and *Ruin, Blossom*, so it made sense to commission the same artist. While preparing this manuscript, the last lines from 'As if from the End Times' seemed to resonate across John's long career and offer an appropriate visual transition, before 'the darkness-to-come'.

Robin Robertson

In memoriam John Burnside
(19 March 1955 – 29 May 2024)

THE EMPIRE OF FORGETTING

NOTES TOWARDS A *DEVOTIO MODERNA*

I

As if there was a sky where we could
pause a while, like medieval
pilgrims, we are patient to the last

and have no thought of After, or the gods
that might have been: the green amidst the black,
the changelings, or the newly resurrected.

Unlike the saints, we have no use
for angels, all that
bright dust floating down

from worlds we have no reason to pursue;
though sometimes, in the house we learned by heart
as children, everaftered in a fog

of Sabbath and the scent of mother love,
we let some devil in to make its bed:
wind in the ashes, chemtrails in the cinders.

We have the dead, their voices calling home
at nightfall; we have
ghost lights on the stairs,

rats in the attic, chipped bowls full of eggs,
but no one here has miracles to tell,
or not, that is, beyond the simple fact

of birch woods, or the first snow of the year,
or, somewhere down the river, where the reeds
are thickest, one last

warbler calling out
from everywhere, a warbler in the dusk,
and then an owl, first

one thing, then the next, and everything
so close to unison, we bow our heads
and call it prayer, as if all things were One.

II

Never a fall, these autumns lead us back
to elsewheres we have reason to believe
are ours, though peopled solely with the shapes
of others, neither memories nor ghosts,
but phantoms, nonetheless, as we have been.

Fog on the roads, the harvest gathered in
by lantern-light; our work, if it is work,
accomplished.
Deer at the fence lines,
field mice in the larder

and all the local kingdoms in their
singing, frog
and heron and that clearing where the air
is thick and sweet with rot, not
blackened yet, but tender with the fade

of quince, or damson, strafed into the grass
and bruised to softness by a week of rain,
the wasps grown quick and blind
around that feast, the pigeons
fattened in the hedges, blind with song.

No need to say how gladly we are pledged
to lost and loved.
How still the field is, now the crop is in.
How blue the sky,
now Heaven is foregone.

III

Late in the year
and everything we know has turned
to chrysalis, the gardens blanked
with snow, the houses
floating in the gold
of festival;

but what is winter here,
if not a ploy
to be recused, the business of the heart
too vague
to be forgotten
or remembered?

The dead lie in their sleeves
of gilt and ice, cold
featherings and tongues to set against
our hatcheries
of marrowfat
and yarrow;

and one thing leads, directly,
to another, lustreless
as early picture books:
a gateway to a path,
the path to water,
junkyard lamps reflected in the still

black surface, shadows
flickering away – a bird, a vole –

while somewhere up ahead, just out of reach,
a winter we have yet to comprehend
waits heart-in-hand
to furnish us with wings.

NOTES TOWARDS A *WÄCHTERLIED*

For years we staked our faith on evensong
and medieval paintings where
the angels, if they chose to speak at all,
said nothing that might implicate a god.

Back in the days when everybody slept
through winters such as this, our simple dwellings
drowsed beneath the snow, a sweet
momentum in the far rooms of the house
where nothing was remembered or forgotten.

Strange, now, to be waking to a world
so ill-contrived that nothing ever sings:
rain on the skylight, voices in the roof,
these pretty seraphs, scorched into the walls,
too faint to name, though some of them had wings.

WINTER SUTRA

World is suddener than we fancy it.
                    Louis MacNeice

Let there be light and shadow; let us
wake to something distant in the house:
a flock of wings, some evidence of meadow;
and let us be as sudden as the sudden

cold, this afternoon, when all the town
falls still and, quietly,
from street to street, on every pane of glass,
the frost performs its secret ministry.

Later, after dark, the snow will come,
blowing through the near woods, thick and fast,
and drifting, while we sleep, into the quick
of morning, so it feels like something dreamed,

as sudden as the light across the yards
that picks us out, live signals in the wind,
beguiled by something we have yet to name,
and suddener than habit can imagine.

THE MEMORY WHEEL

I

If I fail to remember the angels, let me be
bedded with such shadows as I glean

from lamplight, in the warmest nook
of Bedlam, white

as apple blossom, whiter than the white
of first snow, when I walked home from the blue

of cinema and all the creatures there
came out to see what moved beneath the stars

as they did, with no After of Before
to speak of, only

witness, bright,
and constant as this house

where no one sleeps,
but everything is dreamèd.

II

¿Y no es nadie la ilusión?
Juan Ramón Jiménez

Gulls in the wind; cicadas; drifted leaves;
the steady click of death watch
beetle in the beams above our heads:
nowhere is more attuned to analogue
than where we lived
and failed to call it home.
Bound to the wheel,
we have no gift
for magic,
and eldritch is no
proxy when the house
is full of presences
and forms unseen,
tatters of *féerique*
and lilac time,
some local instances
of fauna, blanched
and sightless
in that space beneath the floor
where nothing sings.
No remedy for loss, no
cure for rot,
no solace to be found
in mere ideas:
metempsychosis, say, or *presque-vu,*
time running backwards,
or brought to a perfect standstill;

the myth of the stranger, fifth
in a party of four;
The Flower Sermon;
silence;
unforgetting;
but, some days,
when the light comes through the yards
and calls us out, we find the world again
exactly as it was when things began:
small rain
in a stand of black bamboo,
smoke in a doorway,
the lingering scent
of persimmons.
All afternoon, we listen for the next
extinction, faultlines
spindrift in the blood
of others, and that dream of emptiness
that kept us entertained, when things
seemed plausible.
But nothing comes: you say:
only the wind;
only the wind
in a groundswell of drifted leaves,
and so we go on, apprenticed to illusion:
too much to learn,
and nothing too small to forget:
Vesalius, the art of penmanship,
such angels as have fallen
and the ones
who prosper, being
faithful to their god.
Nothing can match

the bodies they infer
from attic windows
streaked with lime and rain,
wild for to hold and altogether
lovely, till they bleed away and leave
the faintest evidence of having been,
all that we thought we owned,
but left to chance:
flaws in the timelapse,
lesions in the fabric,
aporia as modus operandi.

III

It never turns full circle;
but in the end, the place you find
is home,
its shelves of porcelain
and bottled fruit,
the puzzle jar
that speaks of old illusions.
It never spins for long,
but when it does,
the light falls
on the living and the dead
so evenly, their shadows
coincide,
and all our strict forgetting
comes to naught:
the songbirds in the lanes,
the apple yards,
those mornings
when we shivered from our beds
and lit a fire
to magnify the dark.

A THEORY OF SIBERIA

Where someone I was, on one of his better days,
wakes in an Arctic hush and carries on
with no more destination than
an Otherwise:

frost in the birch woods, brittle,
and bright as glass,
ferry boats locked in the ice
a mile from shore,

the other self,
the one who never stops,
born out of wedlock, skilled in the craft
of forgetting:

the other self, not mine, nor anyone's,
kindles a fire on the dock
and waits for spring:
light on the taiga, river birds flocking for miles.

THE EMPIRE OF FORGETTING

I

Out in the field where, once,
we played Dead Man's Fall,

the others are being called
through the evening dusk

– Kenny and Marek, the Corrigans, Alex McClure –
mothers and sisters calling them home for tea

from kitchens warmed with steam and buttered toast,
broth on the hot plate, ham hough and yellow lentils.

Barely a wave, then they're gone, till no one is left,
and the dark from the woods closes in on myself alone,

the animals watching, the older gods
couched in the shadows.

Decades ago, I suppose,
though I cannot be sure.

I have waited here, under the stars,
for the longest time.

II

What if my mother walked home in the grey
of morning, one last day

of berry season, warm dust on a bedroom
mirror, everything

a promise: drift
and stillness

and the gift of things unseen
implicit in the doorway with the scent

of forced chrysanthemums
and sugared plums?

The world would be the world she vanished from
so quietly, some fifty years ago,

but nothing she might find would be
familiar, other than

by inference: a certain turn of phrase,
the way two bodies touch, that momentary

halcyon of everyone
together, voices, singsong in the dark.

LAST DAYS

after Wilhelm Lehmann

Not that we have a science of forgetting,
but some of us are growing more adept
at hospice, *Tod als Freund*
and starlight at the far end of the ward
where time has stopped, the way it sometimes stops
in theatres, when the actors leave the stage.

Strange, how it seems less story than we once
imagined, how the names and dates get lost
and what we do recall is incidental:
a cracked jug by the bed, October rain,

those white chrysanthemums a friend brought round
this morning, fresh, and peppered with the scent
of somewhere in the land, beyond the names,
that brings us home, but never takes us in.

TO THE OLD GODS

I would have spoken sooner, had I known
that they were true,

but all this time I had my own
companions, majorettes

in gold braid, and a borrowed
angel, not quite native to this place

but stolidly adapted to the blue
of winter, ashes blown into the snow,

the post-box on the corner
gloved with frost.

Solstice is done;
and all that's left of them

is strung out on the back roads,
flecked with tar,

and everything they loved
is erstwhile, in the empire of forgetting:

the animals reduced
to bone, a stink pit

reeking in some recess of the wind
where, once, the hearth was lit

to signal love,
the cinders warm, the creatures gathered in,

the packed earth decked
with wintersweet and holly.

NATURE STUDY

It might have been a puzzle, or a form
of absence we had yet to comprehend:

nature table, blueprints for a way of being
animal, a brightness still to come

implicit in a clutch of plover's eggs,
a bowl of leaves, a weft of bone and feathers;

and yet we were less present in our world
than snail shells, or a slip

of minnow at the bottom of a jar,
forgotten, iridescent, almost gone,

but dreaming, till the end,
of light and rain.

VARIATIONS ON 'THE RUIN'

Home after years,
I was driving the country roads,
passing through land
that should have seemed
familiar:

> *Merry it is in the good greenwood,*
> *When the mavis and merle are singing*

High summer. Just past noon.
I pulled in by a ruined
thicket, sump oil
rotting in the grass, a spill
of Roundup in a rut of mud and dock.

> *Merry it is . . .*

No greenwood here,
just scrub and broken trees,
but something about the light
compelled me, like those TV
crime shows, where the tragic history
is larger than the scene:
depths in the bush where
the missing perfect
their silence, the lost and abandoned
ebbing away so slowly, you could think of them
as ghosts.

I parked the car and found
a starred path through a fly-tipped

midden-land of bones
and rubble, scraps
of calico and lumber, plastic
wrapping and a bale

of fence-wire scabbed with rust,
a simmer beneath it all, of something
animate, but not quite
lifelike, shifts
of chafe and fester
breeding in the dirt.

I pressed on through the wood. At length,
the shadows deepened and I stepped into
what must have been
a homestead, once, a local
theatre of nurture and belonging,
ruined now,   *Eorðgrap hafað*
and almost overgrown: spilt   *waldend wyrhtan forweorone,*
                                                 geleorene,
brickwork patched with red   *heardgripe hrusan, oþ hund*
                                                 cnea
valerian, the hollow   *werþeoda gewitan. Oft þæs*
                                               wag gebad
phantom of a doorframe, pools   *ræghar ond readfah rice æfter*
                                               oþrum,
of slate and cinder, sherds   *ofstonden under stormum;*
                                               steap geap gedreas.

of window glass
– and blossom, blossom,
rising through the ghost
foundations:
foxgloves, purple

loosestrife, sprawls
of clematis and Kiftsgate
roses, speedwell, pyracantha,
creeping phlox

> *trumpet-vine,*
> *fox-glove, giant snap-dragon, a salpiglossis that has*
> *spots and stripes; morning-glories, gourds,*
> *or moon-vines trained on fishing-twine*
> *at the back door;*
> *cat-tails, flags, blueberries and spiderwort,*
> *striped grass, lichens, sunflowers, asters, daisies —*
> *yellow and crab-claw ragged sailors*
> *with green bracts — toad plant,*
> *petunias, ferns; pink lilies, blue*
> *ones, tigers; poppies; black sweet-peas . . .*

The house itself
was lost, its people
gone into the earth, the stonework
moss-grey and mottled red, the mortar
broidered with stonecrop
and spleenwort, footings
drowned in ivy . . .

And that was all. I stood there
for a while,
not animal enough
to feel at home, but
knowing I belonged:

> *seah on sinc, on sylfor, on searogimmas,*
> *on ead, on æht, on eorcanstan,*

>   on þas beorhtan burg bradan rices.
>   Stanhofu stodan, stream hate wearp
>   widan wylme; weal eall befeng
>   beorhtan bosme, þær þa baþu wæron,
>   hat on hreþre. þæt wæs hyðelic.
>   Leton þonne geotan . . .
>   ofer harne stan hate streamas
>   un . . .
>   . . . þþæt hringmere hate
>   . . . þær þa baþu wæron.
>   þonne is . . .
>   . . . re; þæt is cynelic þing,
>   huse . . . burg . . .

A live thing, still, still
creaturely, and liable
to flourish:

>   ewig . . . ewig . . .
>   ewig . . . ewig . . .

A VARIATION ON 'PANIS ANGELICUS'

Panis angelicus
fit panis hominum
        Aquinas

Because they've had nothing to say
since the quattrocento,
the angels have turned
to card tricks
and sleight of hand,
music, but no alleluias, that gleam in the orchard
paling to reveal
a godless calm.

They like it better now, a simple life
of wind and fire,
footprints in the dew
like hieroglyphs, but nothing to reveal
beyond the quiet of another
morning: first light, birdsong through the trees.

A VARIATION ON 'AULD LANG SYNE'

From now on, you should treat me as a hostile
witness, neither
pro nor con, nor

anywhere between;
                      heretical
in every house
but one.

A grown child in the close and holy
darkness, I will
have no business here:

no dolphin run, no cup o' kindness yet,
no good folk westering home
in summer fog.

My ghosts are laid
in veins of anthracite
and firedamp, in the pages of no book,

oxlike and unremarked, beneath a town
that wears its hauntings
quietly and well.

No *wede awa* for me. No *neiges d'antan*.
With every breath
I study to be quiet.

A RECUSANT

If anyone should ask,
tell them I lived
in times of hidden war
on hidden war,
lying alone for years
in cluttered rooms,
my mind tuned
to a tape loop of the bells
at Chion-in.
I never fed the dogs;
now they are gone
– far in the hills, no doubt,
and feral, hunting
lambs and smaller dogs
for blood and sport –
and yet, if someone asks,
say I believed,
a locked soul
in a time of great migrations,
and, sometimes,
when these quarters most recall
the world I learned
in childhood, furniture
and folk songs
and the Book of Common Prayer,
I close my eyes
to let the angels in
in lieu of God,
to bind me with Amen.

THE ELDERS

strait is the gate, and narrow is the way, which leadeth unto life, and few there be that find it
                                        The Gospel of Matthew

I

Clinical as angels, or the frost
in Nunavut,
they peer out from the ice
and find you
wanting, with your bitumen and rapture.

Late in the summer,
baskets of windfall plums
by the kitchen door,
light in the stairwell,
silence and empty mirrors,

but rapture never comes,
only the lull
of bramble season, children on the road
too far from town
to hope they might be saved

by police work,
or the usual forms of prayer;
and those who straggle home are so much
lovelier
for being gone so long

that none of them can enter at the gate
and be resumed,
as if they only came
the long way round, like pilgrims, or the blest,
rings on their fingers, daisies in their hair.

II

Where they might be today
is anyone's guess,

a circle of stones
in a clearing, a pot on the fire,

light through the trees
like somebody's dream

of Valhalla.
What memories they have

of Isfahan
or shadows on the streets

of Nineveh,
they will not speak of

now, home after years
of silk road, ransom, refuge in the dark

with animals
they could not see to name.

Snow falls on the yards.
They leave no tracks.

They call from lane to lane,
but no one hears.

FOLK STORY

Out on the land, where, sometimes,
geese are swans,

and ravens share a logic nothing else
can follow,

the young man is not schooled
in treachery

and speaks to no one, other than the bird
that speaks only to him:

a redwing, or a rarer form
of bunting.

Back in his father's time, there was a way
of keeping secrets

safe, a woman
living out her days in attic rooms,

to spite the parish
she was spinstered in,

and grassmen from the uplands, splicing trees
to build such shelters as might house their dead:

shadows like them, with hearts and working dreams,
who loved too well and could not stoop to guile.

OCTOBER 2023

First hard frost. The old gods gone to ground
in drystane walls and silted
ditchworks, sleet
in squalls along the ridge,
then nothing: silence;
grey on grey on grey.
I walk out to the far edge of the yard
and stare into the distance, almost
sure that I am seen
by all I know is there
and cannot see:
echoed, in a line of stunted gorse
along the hedge-line; noticed, then dismissed
as not quite animal enough
to hunt, or fear.
No gods to speak of
here, but there are
phantoms from an early travelogue
who visit now and then; laying no claim
to worship, they are
kindred to the birds
in field guides: tender, indisputable,
and apparitions all, though they are blessed
as I am, when the first sun filters through
the windbreak, and, in spite of all I know,
the light comes clear
and everything is true.

AS IF FROM THE END TIMES

(Homage to David Garnett)

When all the books are gone, there will be
nothing to remember but a single
porch light at the far end of the road,
where something live is moving in the snow,
a woman, or a fox, it's hard to say.

Last day of birdsong; salt rain in the trees;
the echo of someone going about
their business, making good or making hay
– you never know for sure, although you know
that something here is coming to an end:

last day of weather, lanternlight crossing the yards,
last of those stories our kinfolk used to tell
of woman into fox, fox into deer,
deer into shadow and, always, the darkness-to-come.

GOD BLESS THE CHILD

Of fathering, so little can be said
that carries weight in this, or any world:

the firstborn in his caul
of ravensdown,

the second, *à capella* from the realm
of mole and sphagnum.

Later, they repent and come to heel
so gladly that the whole house swells with pride,

a gown for her,
a morning coat for him,

lambswool and satin, midnight blue
and gold,

an ounce of civet
stitched through every seam.

LISTEN WITH MOTHER

A great hall I could liken it to; with windows letting in strange lights; and murmurs and spaces of deep silence. But somehow into that picture must be brought, too, the sense of movement and change. Nothing remained stable long. One must get the feeling of everything approaching and then disappearing, getting large, getting small, passing at different rates of speed past the little creature; one must get the feeling that made her press on, the little creature driven on as she was by growth of her legs and arms, driven without her being able to stop it, or to change it, driven as a plant is driven up out of the earth, up until the stalk grows, the leaf grows, buds swell. That is what is indescribable, that is what makes all images too static, for no sooner has one said this was so, than it was past and altered.

Virginia Woolf

I

No Aquitaine so distant as the blue
of lamplight at the edge of Brewster's Yard:
it's sixty years ago; I'm eight years old,
a lost boy on the farm road, hoping to be
animal: a lone wolf coming home
to hop the fence, a wildcat in a beam
of torchlight, barely seen, then

gone

       then seen again;

and something else was with me in the dark;
spirits were in the land, but
no one's ghost

> *for, had they been there,*
> *out behind the yards,*
> *I would have seen them in their*
> *gloves and scarves*
> *dusted with moonshine and frost*
> *for the Great Beyond*

threads of light
and carbon in the grass,
woodbine, sorrel, older gods than mine,
but none for worship, small rain in the leaves,
the echo of the sound
inside the sound.

It might have happened here, no way of knowing;
a purer weather, sparrows in the gutters,
that sound the rain makes, streaming through the trees.

I might have been a child; there might have been
a father rising early in the dark
to light a fire . . .

Soon he will be gone into the traffic,
his last steps through the scullery a trail
of Players N°6 and coal-tar soap.

The time is a quarter to two.
Are you sitting comfortably?
Then I'll begin.

Though this is not the tale I bargained for,
and no one calls it home when all the birds
have gone, the last of them
so recent, they left songlines in the trees:
rook and starling, chiffchaff, peregrine.
House martins skim through the fog
on the Old Perth Road,
but only in my sleep, the first bus
idling at the end of Stenhouse Street,
colliers and lampmen turning out
for dayshift, faces
pitted with dismay
and anthracite.

First light in the empire of forgetting,
the morning dusk, that blue between the houses,

owls in the beechwoods, lamplight through the trees,
a horse in its traces, a ton weight of slumber and warmth.

Beyond our lane, a mile of rot and perish,
weasels and adders shivering through a stand
of willow-herb, or Himalayan balsam.
Kids from the prefabs, tinkers, ne'er-do-wells,
pit-town brats in hand-me-downs
and sandshoes . . .

I liked us best when we were still
Implausible:
summer Sundays, going in to Mass,
the chancel splashed with light, the scent
of olibanum, mistle thrush and blackbird
calling back and forth across
the gardens at the end of Stenhouse Street;
that gloaming in the corridors at home time,
stick bouquets of dock and campion,
paper moons of Honesty in seed
unflaking on a table by the door;
or weekdays after school, scouting the Old Perth Road
for jam-jars and bottles,
rinsing them out at the tap
by Brewster's Yard,
and hauling them down
to the Co-op, to claim the deposit.

> *mares eat oats*
> *and does eat oats*
> *and little lambs*
> *eat ivy*

The wireless forever tuned
to HOME, the signal
wavering into the dark
over North Utsire.
Berne. Algiers. Poznań. Hanover.
I knew where nothing was,
but it was there:
the privet lanes; the woods;
High Valleyfield.
The miles of snow
to Kraków and Bokhara.
Summer in Cape Town;
mid-afternoon in Nagoya.

Are you sitting comfortably?

That house was never mine. Mine was the hum of blowflies in the attic, micro-spills of vinegar and rice, the hush of what was holy in its day, stamps and Mass cards pressed between the pages of the gospel

> *— my mother at the table, gloved with flour,*
> *the elsewhere in her eyes too bright to fathom —*

I never asked for hymnals, only a charm of finches, flitting away from here to where the neighbours lived in blessed incognito.

Shore birds on fresh-ploughed fields, in from the coast to forage, sanderling and curlew, redshank and black-backed gull. A first gleam over No-Man's-Land, where the Perth Road skirted the prefabs —

> *There was something I wanted to say, some word from a fairy tale,*
> *or maybe a prayer, rephrased by the wind in an empty stairwell.*

Caught between church
and gospel, thinking in tongues,
I waited for *a rushing mighty wind*
to flood the house, first
portent of a minor Pentecost.
On its shelf in the back press, sacred,
untouched for years,
my grandfather's Bible
slept in its cradle of dust:
the book as fetish, not the word of God,
but glue and paper, leather, printer's ink,
the fly-leaf flecked with dander, pages greased
with brilliantine and microdots of coal.
It stood for something; what, I never knew;
my mother had her own grimoire
of charms and simples, spells cast in the lamplit
scullery, the gold light on her hands
of GEC – *a kid'll eat ivy too, wouldn't you?* –
That absence in the doorway where her voice
had faltered, but an absence I could hear.
Mornings, when the milk-cart made its rounds,
she stepped out to the litmus of the frost:
the farm road fogged with breath, the drayhorse
dreamlike behind its blinkers, Beath Woods
hovering above them, limned with snow.
Some days, I followed her out
and watched, as she stroked the mane,
a gravity pulling her in
to the larger presence.

> *Out in the dark, over the snow*
> *the owls are hunting field mice, purely*

*watchful, like the wind-smoothed
graves along the coast, forgotten
ferrymen and creelers gusting home
as fledgling spectres, howling from a scrim
of moss and stone –*

II

All the way home, we saw it from the train:
land that belonged to no one, a pagan darkness
looming through the beechwoods, shadows streaming
headlong through a field of oats or barley;
the lives of others, hunkered between the stations,
silos, bonfires, dairies, timber yards;
place names a hair's breadth away
from another tongue,
darkness and holy wells, a thousand years
of solemn hunters, coming through the trees;
pit towns blurred with smoke, the headframes stalled;
barnyard roses clenched against the rain.

NOTES & ACKNOWLEDGEMENTS

Notes Towards a *Devotio Moderna*

Devotio Moderna: a late-medieval religious movement that emphasised the inner spiritual life of the individual and encouraged a more personal attitude towards belief and religion.

Notes Towards a *Wächterlied*

Wächterlied ('The Guardian's Song') by Edvard Grieg, Opus 12. Its subtitle was 'Composed after a performance of Shakespeare's Macbeth'.

The Memory Wheel

féerique: magical, fairy-like; as in a fairy-tale
presque-vu: literally 'almost-seen'; on the brink of epiphany
The Flower Sermon: a story of the origin of Zen Buddhism in which the Buddha transfers direct wisdom to the disciple via a lotus flower
Vesalius: anatomist, physician, famous for his book of woodcuts of human anatomy, *De Humani Corporis Fabrica Libri Septem* (1543)
aporia: a perplexing difficulty

A Theory of Siberia

taiga: the swampy coniferous sub-Arctic forest; also known as the snow forest

The Empire of Forgetting

Dead Man's Fall: Scottish children's game involving simulated execution. The most dramatic 'death' wins.

ham hough: ham hock, a hind-leg joint of meat
halcyon: a period of calm

Last Days

Tod als Freund: 'Death as a Friend', a wood engraving by Alfred Rethel, 1851

To the Old Gods

wintersweet: winter marjoram

Variations on 'The Ruin'

'Merry it is in the good greenwood, When the mavis and merle are singing' is from *The Lady of the Lake* by Walter Scott

The original Old English –

'*Eorðgrap hafað
waldend wyrhtan forweorone, geleorene,
heardgripe hrusan, oþ hund cnea
werþeoda gewitan. Oft þæs wag gebad
ræghar ond readfah rice æfter oþrum
ofstonden under stormum; steap geap gedreas.*'

– might be loosely translated as: 'Earth-grip holds the master-builders, departed now, perished and fallen in the hard grasp of earth, while a hundred generations of people have passed. Long had this wall – lichen-grey and stained with red – lasted through one reign after another, withstanding the storms, but this high arch has finally fallen.'

And the other section of Old English, with its *lacunae* –

'. . . seah on sinc, on sylfor, on searogimmas,
on ead, on æht, on eorcanstan,
on þas beorhtan burg bradan rices.
Stanhofu stodan, stream hate wearp
widan wylme; weal eall befeng
beorhtan bosme, þær þa baþu wæron,
hat on hreþre. Þæt wæs hyðelic.

Leton þonne geotan
ofer harne stan hate streamas
un . . .
. . . þþæt hringmere hate
þær þa baþu wæron.
þonne is
. . . re; þæt is cynelic þing,
huse . . . . . burg . . . .

is approximately: '. . . gazed on treasures of silver and gold, on precious stones, wealth and in that radiant city of broad dominion.

Stone courts once stood here, wide streams welled up hot from their source, surrounded by a wall so the baths were heated at the heart. Hot streams ran over hoar stone into the pool . . . it is a kingly thing, a house . . . city . . .'

The third italic section – '*the trumpet vine . . . black sweet-peas . . .*' – is from 'The Steeple-Jack' by Marianne Moore.

The German word *ewig* means 'forever'.

A Variation of 'Auld Lang Syne'

firedamp: flammable gas, especially methane, found in coalmines

'*wede awa*': the refrain from the famous lament for the dead of Flodden —'*The Flowers of the Forest are a' wede awa*' — can be Anglicised as 'withered away'.
neiges d'antan: snows of yesteryear (Villon)

A Recusant

'Chion-in': the Buddhist 'Monastery of Gratitude' in Higashiyama-ku, Kyoto, Japan

The Elders

'Nunavut': the largest and northernmost territory of Canada, forming most of the Canadian Arctic Archipelago
'Isfahan': city in central Iran, known for its Persian architecture

Listen with Mother

The epigraph is from Woolf's *Moments of Being*
'dander': the vitrified refuse of a smith's fire or a furnace; a calcined cinder or piece of slag
'grimoire': a manual for invoking spirits
'headframes': a framework on top of a mine-shaft or pit

*

'A Recusant' and 'Winter Sutra' were first published in the *London Magazine*.
Many of these poems first appeared in the *London Review of Books*: 'Notes towards a *Devotio Moderna*', parts I and II of 'The Memory Wheel', part I of 'The Empire of Forgetting' (as 'The Persistence of Memory'), 'A Variation on "Panis Angelicus"' and 'God Bless the Child'. With thanks to Jean McNicol.